# WHERE DID MY INDUSTRY GO?

**Why once successful Estate and Letting Agencies are struggling and how a new dawn can turn them back into great businesses.**

## Mark Burgess

**therealmarkburgess.co.uk**

Growbag Publishing
Turtle farm
South End
Hertfordshire
SG10 6EP

Print version ISBN: 978-1-5272-1605-1
Ebook version ISBN: 978-1-5272-1620-4

# CONTENT MARKETING

-The 5Cs -

Content

Communicate

Connect

Constant

Convert

# Why Me, Why You?

Let's face it, not many people out there like estate or letting agents. But I have some good news for you. I do.

Both my current business and I personally have worked with hundreds, if not bordering on thousands of agents, during the course of more than 20 years. I have worked: as an agent; as an advisor to agents; and I have helped countless agents to gain a better understanding of their business and techniques used in other sectors to help them improve their companies.

Why did I write this book and who is it for? During the years I have come to know hundreds of agents in the United Kingdom, Europe and around the world. And the vast majority of them I get on really well with; but why? This is a question I have asked myself many times. The answer is that, although I have 20+ years of experience in marketing, publishing and digital marketing, my first true love was estate agency. Corny, I know, but true. And as any experienced agents out there will know, once that is in you, it never really goes away.

Okay sure, I discovered other passions along the road. I love technology and think up new concepts that use that technology to solve problems for people in business. But, in one way or another, I always find myself applying those solutions to estate and letting agency businesses.

I wrote this book to help people in the property agency sector to have a better understanding of where their beloved industry has gone and why their once thriving business sometimes feels like it is coming apart at the seams.

Of course, I am not ashamed to admit that one of my businesses is directly involved in helping to solve these issues for estate and letting agents. But regardless of that, if my knowledge can 'turn on the lights' for someone in the same way that I have seen it happen so many times in my face-to-face meetings, or seminars during the years, that would be the real win for me.

Most of the agents who I know would openly admit that, while specialists in their sector, they know very little about the world of social media, digital marketing, tracking, automation and such like. This is where I can help, by providing you with this book.

This book is for the owners of estate and letting agents who can see the world changing around them and are feeling a little lost as to what they should do about it. Why? Because this book can reach people faster than I can go around and speak to people individually, thus helping more people, more quickly, before it is too late.

If you have read to this point and are interested, then this book is for you. It provides you with a clearer understanding of exactly how to market your business in today's world and what you should and should not be spending your time and effort on.

# What Other Agents Are Saying About The Author

*"When we first set up a meeting on content marketing with Mark I really had no idea what it meant, I just knew that it sounded like a subject that our company should embrace. Mark was able to explain the precise strategy behind content marketing and why it should be a major component in our overall marketing strategy. He helped us understand the full circle of nurturing data to its maximum."*

**Mark Cooper, Partner, Coopers Estate Agents**

*"Within a 20 minute meeting with Mark I understood with ease and in great depth the whole point of digital content marketing. He explained it in a completely non-techie capacity and within seconds Mark could demonstrate with simple hand drawn flow charts (on demand) the journey the end user would take and the commercial benefits to our company. This started with brand awareness right through to the perception of being the expert and therefore, ultimately the only company a client would consider using for services by an almost subliminal and unconscious strategy."*

**Ben Bird, Company Owner, Sterling Property Group**

*"I have had the pleasure of speaking to Mark on a few occasions, he has a relaxed, assured and straightforward manner, which has helped me get a better grasp on an area I confess is outside of my comfort zone. But one that I can see has an increasing importance and relevance to my industry. Mark has helped us clarify our thinking and make a breakthrough in terms of marketing our business."*

**Andrew Gilchrist, MD for Frosts and Lawlors, part of the LSLi Group**

*"Before we spoke to Mark about content marketing and how the whole content marketing loop works, we had no idea about that specific form of marketing. Working with Mark has been great for our business and I highly recommend him."*

**John Wagstaff, Director, Petty Son and Prestwich**

*"We have been working with Iceberg for the last five years and during this time our business has gone from strength to strength. We are now market leaders in most of the towns we operate in and regularly win prestigious awards."*

**Martin Gibbon, Managing Director, Balgores Group**

"*We are very pleased with the progress we have made. Through the use of FRAGRA, a quarterly personalised newspaper and other marketing material we have managed to double the level of valuations we have generated since the beginning of the year. We are committed to our continued growth in sales and we very much see Iceberg Digital playing a significant role in achieving our goals.*"

**Marlon Fox, Managing Director, Outlook Property**

"*Working with Iceberg Digital is a big commitment as these guys are not just in it for the short haul. The longer term strategic planning was something missing from my business and they solved that problem for me 110%.*"

**Neil King, Managing Director, Neil King Residential**

# WHERE DID MY INDUSTRY GO?

# About the Author

Mark Burgess is the CEO of Iceberg Digital, a UK based business, which provides: educational, engaging and entertaining content; social media management; tracking systems; lead nurturing; and marketing, through a unique suite of products for the property industry. He has more than 20 years of experience in the property, marketing, publishing and digital marketing industry and has managed numerous successful businesses.

Iceberg Digital has hundreds of clients; an international office; and has won many technology and digital marketing awards - but more importantly - they have helped hundreds of their clients to win prestigious awards as well.

Mark is a regular speaker at numerous national and international events in the property sector such as; The Negotiator Conference; The Hunters National and International Conference; and he is highly regarded by his peers and colleagues as an expert in his field.

Leaving school with no formal qualifications, Mark is one of life's true non-conformers. He attempts to reshape and remould everything he encounters, sometimes with huge frustration; but often with great success. Mark has been a business owner and entrepreneur from the age of 24 and has experienced the dark times, as well as the great times that vocation can bring.

During his school life, Mark was a top-level student but could not bring himself to conform to a system he did not believe in. He was singled out as trouble and at the time, he was seen as a drop out; a student of great potential, but with no application. However, this trait has proven to be his greatest asset in life and business. His ability to think outside of the box, create his own rules and his need to improve existing processes has led to his many business successes.

# Acknowledgements

My beautiful wife Hayley who is also my best friend, business partner and lover. Everything I do is so we can spend more time with each other; that is my true, real passion. Work, systems, money; they are all a by-product of wanting to achieve that goal.

My wonderful son Fraser and my princess daughter Grace. You are more special to me than you will ever understand. This book is my gift to you guys, read it, learn it and understand it. Your school can teach you many things but hopefully, so can your old Dad too!

My Mum and my Dad. My parents separated when I was five and although I am sure they went through difficult times, they never let me or my brother see that. They are both great people and I hope I can treat my kids with the same respect you guys gave me.

Rosemary Georges, the Mum of my best friend at school. I spent many days and nights at her home. Rose taught me so many things without knowing it. Rose worked as a nurse for the National Health Service and worked what seemed to me at the time, to be night shifts, day shifts and everything-in-between shifts. Rose showed me another side to life - that hard work does not always pay - and that life is not always fair. Rose, if you are reading this; you are a true legend, one of the greatest people I ever met. Thank you.

My book coach and editor, Wendy Yorke, for helping me to make this book a reality.

# Foreword

"From the many years I have known Mark, he has never failed to impress me with how he strives to continually develop both personally and in his business. At a time when most people were still committed to print, Mark was way ahead of the curve in understanding the benefits of digital marketing.

His business was then, one of the first in the property industry to pioneer many new ideas with advanced online campaigns and so it was of no surprise to me that he was an early adopter in understanding and developing his skills in content marketing. It is entirely down to his passion and belief in how content marketing has evolved, that he convinced me to act on his recommendations with some degree of urgency! We live in a fast developing world.

As a business owner I need quality guidance from trusted advisors who can positively impact on my company. Mark has continually achieved this during the years and in particular, had an illuminating impact on my understanding of the need to adjust to the complete and important journey that content marketing offers.

Mark's knowledge on the whole subject and its benefits are second to none and I would urge any SME owner who is serious about their future development and growth, to read this book, talk with Mark and to listen and act."

**Andrew Dickinson, Director, Oakwood Homes**

# Contents List

# CHAPTER 1
## Estate Agency, The Good Old Way

**"Estate agency is currently sitting at a crossroads.
In one direction, they can follow the high street greengrocer
- in the other direction - is a world of exceptional growth
and the reinvention of an entire industry."**

My first experience of agency was back in the mid 1990s. I was fresh out of an education that had ended prematurely - of my own accord - leaving me with precisely no qualifications of any note. I had bounced around a couple of dead end jobs before I was introduced to estate agency through a friend.

I attended an interview in my newly purchased suit and I met with the Area Manager and Branch Manager of an up and coming estate agency chain, called Spicer McColl.

I was as keen as could be in my interview and I got the job on the grand annual salary of £5,000 per annum plus commission. Little did I know that my enthusiasm was merely a bonus for the management team at Spicer McColl. Their rapid growth meant that the only real requirement needed to fill the position was simply a working pulse.

## Hit the ground running

I had my first position in an agency, and boy was it an experience! The first branch where I worked was in Newham, East London. From that office we worked across the entire Borough. For those of you not familiar with Newham, it is one of London's poorest areas. The population is diverse, but at the time was mainly made up of three main demographics. There were traditional, white English people who had lived there all of their lives; there were Indians who had moved to the UK within the last few years; and there were also Africans who were new to the country. Although diverse, the area was not well integrated and there were 'pocket' areas where each of these demographics felt secure.

My manager at the time was called Peter Bowerman. Pete was around 10 years older than me and knew the area and the working of it inside out. Pete was actually a great influence on my life; not only from the point of view of how to negotiate a sale and fix the issues required to see that sale through to exchange. But Pete actually taught me things he perhaps did not even know he was teaching me. And to be fair I did not know he was teaching me either until 20 years later!

Our office was a corner office on a busy junction in the middle of town. I can still remember my first week in that office. I had not worked there more than a few days before Saturday arrived and at various points during the week I had found myself in the office alone, dealing with telephone enquiries and walk in customers and feeling completely out of my depth. But I survived. Not only did I survive, I kind of loved it; in the same way as a really tough gym session or run. There was nothing pleasurable about it at the time, but once the day was done I felt kind of important, like people had needed my help and I had given it to them.

Our agency at the time did not have computers on each desk. We did have one computer for the secretary in the corner of the office, but it was a scary machine, which only she knew how to use.

For the front line we each had two essential tools for our trade. The first was our applicant box. A small rectangular box much like a small ice-cream carton that sat proudly on your desk. The box was what made you special. Inside this box were your completed registrations of potential buyers and they belonged to you and you alone.

Like a game of poker, when a newly listed property came on to the market each negotiator in the office scanned the data banks of their mind and flicked through their applicant box to 'match' the perfect buyer to the property, before anyone else could. Although only cards with information on them, each card almost had it's own face and personality in your mind, regardless of if you had actually met the person face-to-face or only ever spoken to them on the telephone.

It was key that you understood the needs of as many people in your applicant box as possible to match them with the right properties. And, through more and more conversations you built true rapport with these people, your customers, eventually finding many of them their perfect property.

This side of the business was always fun. You were helping people. It was not your fault if what they were looking for was not available, but you were offering your insight and knowledge to try and help them overcome their problem of finding a specific type of property. However, all those who have worked in agency know, this was not the most important part of the business from a management perspective.

## On the job training

The key to being a successful office for the management was actually getting people to put their property on the market with your agency. Therefore, only the most trusted staff would be assigned the role of 'valuer' and allowed to go out and win the new business.

Interestingly, this side of the business was less fun. It was still a thrill but it was a different kind of enjoyment. It was based on the fact that you had beaten your competition to sealing the deal of who the seller chose to sell their property. It was also based around how well you convinced the seller to pay a large agency fee. It was a polar opposite to the idea of helping potential buyers solve their problems for free. Instead, we were selling a set service for as much as we could.

It felt like we were some kind of sharp-suited Wall Street traders, on the hunt for the next big fee, winning the business at all costs. In reality, we were relatively low qualified, cheap-suited guys, offering not much in particular for a reasonably large sum of someone's money.

When I say low qualified, we were certainly not unskilled. To walk into a stranger's home and walk out with a signed contract for them to give you thousands of pounds in less than the time it takes to cook a roast chicken is pretty impressive. Training was provided, but it was not the type of training that was followed through to completion, it was more a *Hints and Tips Guide,* which you could use if you needed to. Rather than a fundamental structure of how the business should be run and conducted. Everything else was learnt on the job and as such came down to experience.

I went on to work in all different 'types' of estate agency offices; high-end and mid-range. I also did a stint as a mortgage advisor, so I could understand that side of the business better. But in each office, the process was essentially the same.

## The crossroads

During the years hundreds of staff who experienced that exact same process have gone on to open their own estate or letting agency and implemented - pretty much - the same system. Yes, the advent of computers and Rightmove have changed parts of the process, but have they really made all that much difference to the bottom line or indeed the process?

In the more than twenty years since leaving my roles in estate agency I have built various businesses. All but one of them have stayed connected to the estate and letting agency business in some way or another, but they have not been estate agencies themselves. Instead, my background has been in marketing, publishing and early adoption of pushing the boundaries of the digital age. In this book my goal is to help thousands of estate and letting agents who really want to do a good job, but have never had the opportunity to learn the blueprints of how to do effective content marketing in this current age.

Estate agency is currently sitting at a crossroads. In one direction, they can follow the high street greengrocer - in the other direction - is a world of exceptional growth and the reinvention of an entire industry. This book is designed to help you turn the right way. But before you start, I ask one thing. Rather than trying to disagree or disprove all or any of my theories, give yourself a chance to see the benefits of them - after all, you have absolutely nothing to lose - and the possibility of **everything** to gain.

# CHAPTER 2
## The Worrying New Dawn

**"The online model of estate agency is a great example of how many agents are simply reactive to whatever their competition is doing. They see someone having success with a particular model or service and they think, great we need to do that too."**

Market conditions for estate and letting agencies will always be influenced hugely by outside economic and social events. Because of this fact, there is really, very little point in you or I taking these events into account when looking at how to make your business more successful.

If the economic or social events happening to you while you are reading this book are such that nothing anyone says or does can help your business, then it is worth reading on because you will find the information useful for your next business venture. If however, your business is still standing and more importantly still swinging punches at this point, then this book will help put you right back in the match.

## What is the point of your business?

You can give the simple answer, which states who you are and what your business does. For example, to sell or let properties, but actually the question and the answer are much more complex than that. To get the most out of this mini exercise, I want you to give yourself a moment of clarity. Disassociate yourself with all of the emotion and hard work you put into your business day in and day out. I acknowledge that your business is your baby, but for five minutes lose your 'protectiveness' of your baby and take a large step back.

Now, pride-denting as this might be - comparing the various estate and letting agencies operating in your town - what is the point of your business? If it were to disappear tomorrow, what problem would your potential customers not be able to solve?

Remember the purpose of this is to allow yourself to be vulnerable. This is only a conversation happening inside your head, so there is no point in coming up with weak reasons such as; "Well, if we weren't around they would miss our customer service" or "We work really hard." While these types of reasons help to make a great business, these sorts of statements alone do not make a business. The majority of estate and letting agencies are first and foremost struggling with the issue of providing almost identical offerings to their competition.

## Playing in a field of one

*"If you can recognise competition as a destructive force instead of a sign of value, you're already more sane than most"*
**Peter Thiel, founder of PayPal and author of Zero to One**

Peter Thiel shows us a good example of the brutal competition. While US airlines serve millions of passengers and create hundreds of billions of dollars of value each year, they make only 37 cents per passenger per trip. On the other hand, Google has one hundred times higher profit margin than all other airline industries.

Capitalism means capital. Competition means there would be no capital for you, the pie will be eaten by the other players. To increase your capital you need to be a monopolist and escape the competition.

You may argue that monopolies are bad, but this is true only in a world where nothing changes. In our world, it's possible to invent new and better ways of doing business. Creative monopolists give customers more choices by adding entirely new categories of products.

When I first read this and applied the theory to my own business, it annoyed me and left me thinking; "Well, good for you Peter Thiel, but unfortunately for me we can't all come up with PayPal! Some of us are just trying to make a living." But I was seriously missing the point.

The idea is not that you need to invest in some sort of revolutionary new idea that has never been thought of before, but more that you need to rethink your strategy. You need to step off the hamster wheel for long enough to take a look and say; "What kind of estate agency needs to be invented to solve a problem no one else is solving?"

With simply a few minutes of focused thought the ideas can suddenly start to flow. Some of your ideas will be unworkable ideas for one reason or another and some ideas will merit further investigation.

For example;
- Why don't estate agencies organise customer removals?
- Why don't estate agencies offer a refurbishment service before marketing for properties in need of repair?
- Why don't letting agencies take quarterly video footage of their property inspections to send to the landlord?
- Why don't agents have monthly face-to-face meetings with their sellers?

These are ideas I thought up in less than five minutes. I am not claiming any of them to be the answer for you or your business, but hopefully they help bring you away from the feeling that your business has no point when compared with the competition. And instead, it is actually only simple changes that need to be made for you to go from playing in a field swamped with competition, to playing in a field of one.

## Task: What is your strategy?

Spend a few minutes writing a list of your ideas to improve the estate and letting agency industry. View it from a new angle and see what you can come up with. However, if you struggle don't worry, come back to this task later. The list does not have to be perfect and you do not have to fill in the whole table. This is an ideas task and is intended to get you thinking in the right direction.

# Ideas to improve the estate and letting agency industry

| | |
|---|---|
| 1 | |
| 2 | |
| 3 | |
| 4 | |
| 5 | |
| 6 | |
| 7 | |
| 8 | |

Keep this exercise in mind as you read through this book. As you go through the process of examining and understanding more deeply how to reinvent your business, into your town and surrounding areas, revisit this table to add new ideas to it as and when they pop into your mind.

The online model of estate agency is a great example of how many agents out there are simply reactive to whatever the competition are doing. They see someone having success with a particular model or service and think, great we need to do that too. The problem with that strategy is that it means you don't actually have any strategy!

Go back to the original question. What is the point of your business? If you have a clear reason to exist in the marketplace then you have no need to keep jumping from one idea to the next to keep up with the competition. When you have a clear reason to exist, there is no competition. Sure, other people will offer other services and have their own successes, but this should not worry or deter you from your goals and reasons for being in business. You might even find yourself recommending them when you come across someone who does not need your service.

Let's use the traditional way of charging fees in an estate agency as a great example. Most agents charge a percentage of the selling price for selling a property, but why?

To understand what follows, clear your mind of all past facts you have been taught and just think about it in a simple and logical way.

One customer has an apartment worth £250,000 and at a rate of 1.5% will be charged £3,750 to sell their property. The next customer has a house worth £1.5million and at the same rate of 1.5% they will be charged £22,500 to sell their property. That is one hell of a difference for essentially the same service.

I have had this argument many times with my estate agency friends and clients and usually I receive random standard responses as to why this could ever have been seen as fair. Generic answers such as; "It is harder to sell the more expensive property because there are less buyers" or; "The more expensive property requires extra marketing." But when pushed on what extra marketing or why having fewer buyers to pick from should result in a fee six times that of the apartment sale, there are rarely any decent or logical reasons. For example, if the apartment does take a long time to sell and the £1.5million property sells quickly do the fees reverse? The answer of course is no, so the arguments don't stack up and the fees don't make any logical sense.

Now, don't take this the wrong way. I am not saying that you should not charge £22,500 to sell a property worth £1.5million. You have to be able to quantify how your fee structure works and why. And if you are going to detail the reason why and justify it, it is not good enough to give generic answers. This is what leads to you not really having any set price and everyone feeling as though they can negotiate on your fees. Again, please don't mistake this as me saying 'offer cheap fees' because I am not in favour of that. I am simply saying, explain why you charge what you charge. Give the price and don't negotiate.

For example, perhaps figure out your charging model and establish a cost to:
- advertise a property for sale and conduct viewings for a set period of time;
- for looking after the conveyancing part of the process, up to a set amount of properties in the chain, with further costs for longer chains; and
- for all of the little bits and bobs that make the more difficult sales worth it for you but don't rely on people not asking any hard questions of you.

From these, figure out how many properties you need to sell to turn a good profit and then do it. No need to go crazy trying to get and sell everything. If you can give a reasonable and fair pitch that results in the sale of a property costing the seller £6,000 (this is just an example number I realise this may be high or low depending on your location) then that means you need to sell 100 properties from your branch to turn over £600,000 which is more than most single branches do. You don't need to take everything onto the market. You simply need to find the 100 sellers that are looking for the service you provide for £6,000. It might not be achievable to switch from your current position straight to that overnight, but it can be a one or two year goal.

When you can get that business model to work, then based on the principles of marketing I am about to explain to you in this book, you can build a phenomenal business and exit that business for multi-millions of pounds in the future. And all by simply implementing specific and strategic business goals and stopping to work out whether the actions you are taking in your business are good ideas or are simply ideas that you have inherited from the rest of the industry.

Although thinking of your company's reason to exist won't be easy, it is invaluable and once you have it you will see, actually, it is really not that hard to get instructions at a higher fee than you ever thought possible. All you need to do is find the people who specifically want to solve the problem you can solve!

How do you find those people? Traditionally, marketing in estate and letting agency has been one-dimensional. The general rule of thumb has been to create some form of advertising campaign and drop printed leaflets into as many properties as is affordable, hoping to get a random response from someone in one of those properties who is looking to sell or let.

This approach no longer works. To understand how to solve this issue we first need to understand why it did once work and also what has changed to make it stop working.

# CHAPTER 3
## The Winds of Change

"Actions, which will bring the people who love your product, service or knowledge, right to your door and allow you to not only do what you love but charge a premium for doing it and provide you with happy customers."

For the past quarter of a century the general rules of marketing for small, medium and big businesses have been common knowledge and widely accepted. But with modern technology moving at such a fast pace during the past twenty years and almost at hyper speed in terms of marketing in the last four or five years, the majority of businesses have been left behind. Estate and letting agencies are notoriously slow at adopting new technology.

I, personally, do not believe this is due to any lack of thinking or ability because some of the most forward thinking and inspiring people I know are agents. It seems to me to be more because of the; "If it isn't broken, don't fix it" approach. However, it is becoming clearer and clearer to many that actually...it is broken...although, some agents are yet to realise this!

One thing is for certain - those who can understand how the world, consumers and their potential customers have changed - will triumph and those who cannot accept change or refuse to even investigate it will suffer.

Before we can start to look at how to use a specific content marketing loop in business to drive more leads, we must understand where we have come from. To do that, I am going to give you a brief explanation of the history of interruption marketing.

## Interruption marketing

During the period of the last century interruption marketing has been the basics to build on for every business. At the time, it was not called interruption marketing because there was no other effective method of marketing. Hence it was and still is to the majority, simply known as marketing.

The idea behind interruption marketing is to borrow or rent your potential customer's eyeballs for a short period of time while they are in the process of doing something else. For example, a television advert interrupts the programme that your potential customer is watching, borrowing their eyes for a few moments. A leaflet posted through your door interrupts the process of you walking in and out of your property and magazines, newspapers and radio adverts interrupt your programmes, articles or songs.

**Adverts, which merely shout about your business, no longer work**

This method of marketing was widely accepted as a fair trade off by the public as a means to an end. They wanted free television and therefore had to accept the adverts. In fact, I remember as a child watching the television as a family and the adverts themselves were like an interesting event. Even business owners accepted tactics, such as leaflets and cold calling because they were probably employing those very same tactics themselves in their own business. In estate and letting agencies the best examples of this are things like, having the most For Sale or For Let boards up in your area; having the most advert pages in the local paper; and making sure you keep putting leaflets through the doors of properties in your local area.

It is important not to feel as though I am trying to make this form of marketing sound pointless and dead; far from it. I strongly believe interruption marketing has a place. But it does not have the same place it used to, which was effectively the whole marketing arm of your business. It was lead generation central and an exercise in who could shout the loudest. Otherwise known as share of voice to share of market.

Most small to medium sized businesses do not have the budget to advertise on television. But we can take television as a great example of how times have now changed.

For those of you who are old enough to have experienced a world without mobile telephones and the Internet, try to picture your television viewing experience, when the family sat down to watch a show. What other kinds of distractions were there to take your attention away from the television? The answer is not much! Even if you dared to talk too much, someone would complain and God forbid, if the home telephone was to ring during a television show! An argument would ensue about who the call was likely to be for and who was going to answer it, only for you probably to tell the caller that you would call them back once your show had finished. Now that is true engagement.

Let's compare that with television engagement in today's world. When you finally get a chance to sit down and flick on the television, what other kinds of distractions are there to take your attention away from it? Do you even care what is on? Are you checking your Facebook? Are you sending an SMS text? Are you using it as television viewing time or simply general leisure time to wind down? In an age where no one has enough time and everybody does three or four things at once the television shows we want to watch are usually pre-recorded or downloaded, so we can pick our time for this carefully and skip the adverts and any other interruptions.

Our smartphones allow us to filter out content and read or watch news or entertaining content without the need to have adverts interrupt us. Heck, even a five second advert at the start of a YouTube video has your right index finger twitching, waiting to click the Skip Button at the earliest possible opportunity! I often think to myself, if YouTube ever wanted to get a lot of people to click something they should one day replace that Skip Button. People click it so fast that their clicks would go off the scale! Now imagine how annoying that would be and you are starting to get a real feel for perhaps why the interruption marketing you once knew, trusted and invested in, is no longer working.

In this book, you will learn how best-in-class businesses have overcome this problem for the better and how you can learn and implement some of the strategies so your marketing is no longer like swishing around in the dark, or taking actions because the competition do them. Instead you can be taking action that truly sets you apart, something no one can ever truly copy. Actions, which will bring the people who love your product, service or knowledge, right to your door and allow you - to not only do what you love - but charge a premium for doing it and provide you with happy customers.

Now that you understand what interruption marketing is, it is important for you to also understand the difference between finding potential customers in an active market and finding potential customers in a dormant market.

## Active markets

An active market would be all of those potential customers who are currently considering or using a product or service that your business offers. For most businesses, these are the ones they are trying to find and they generally do this by advertising special offers or telling people about the fantastic products or service they offer. However, there is a huge problem in going after this particular kind of customer and that is price.

Any potential customers who you attract from an active market will either already be comparing your product against several other products that they have researched or may already be using a product that is similar to yours. As a result of these factors your pitch to them is going to quickly move to a discussion about the cost of your products or services and how they compare to the competition. Eventually, winning new business will be because you are the cheapest and will only lead one way - to lots of work - and not much money. Someone will undercut you in the same way you have undercut other businesses and as that is your only unique selling point (USP) your business will crash.

I meet many business owners in various sectors who are convinced the only way of getting more customers is to offer a low fee or a cheap solution. This belief is more prevalent than ever in the estate agency market. The reason this is happening to them is because they keep going after the same kind of customer in the active market.

# Dormant markets

The dormant markets are the potential customers who could use your product or service, but are not currently looking for them. These are the people we want! Why? Because if someone not currently looking to use or buy your product or service decides they like the sound of your business, the conversation is one not based around fees; unless of course you make it that way.

The way to attract clients or customers from the dormant market is not to sell them a sausage, but instead to sell them the sizzle. I was first told this when I worked as a junior estate agent, but as it turns out the people teaching me did not actually understand the concept themselves.

Big businesses understand it so well that you can't escape it in everyday life. But small and medium sized businesses can often struggle to recreate it. The idea is to offer solutions to problems that they need solving. By this I do not mean, the problem is I want to sell my property, for a low fee. If that is the only problem someone has, then helping them is not going to help you build a great business.

To find out their real wants and needs we have to be able to dig deeper into the data of some of our own clients. We will look at exactly how you can do this later in this book because it will be essential in the reinvention of your business.

Top-level businesses sell hundreds if not thousands of their products to people based on the sizzle; the idea that only they can truly give you what you want from life. Sometimes it is hard to see how you can apply that to your business but you can, it simply takes some thinking. Your service or product has a problem in it somewhere that no one else is solving, if you can find that problem and wrap it up into your offering, you can make it incomparable and the question of fees will disappear.

Let's take an estate agent as an example because my business has helped hundreds of those customers during the years. In the UK for the estate agent, it is all about getting the seller to choose you to market their home. To win the business, agents are driving each other's fees down and down and down, to breaking point. They are trying to stand out by offering extra services such as professional photography, or drawing up of floor plans etc. But ultimately, they are going after business in the active market and therefore, having to win most business based on their fees. Very occasionally, they turn up at someone's property only to find that the new client wants to use them exclusively because they have seen their branded For Sale boards, sold a property nearby or a friend's property etc. It is very rare that the agent is not drawn into a conversation about fees and can instead charge their normal fee and have a great day.

But what is the secret in that business that no one is seeing or the problem that no one is solving? How did they manage to take that last property onto the market with no fight about the fees? That happened because the customer wanted to use them exclusively. They wanted to use them because they wanted an easy life and for everything to work and they felt this would happen because the agent had sold their friend's property.

In our modern society, people want an easy life. They already have far too many things to do in the little time they have to do them. Perhaps, rather than going round potential new customer's properties and telling them how you can take professional photos and sell their house or apartment, what if you sit down with them and try to find out what problems it is they are looking to solve? Of course, they will tell you the basic reasons to begin with, but you must be prepared to push them further through your fact and feel finding questioning. To find out how prepared they are for the challenge ahead and what it is that is motivating them.

After they have told you the basic and obvious reasons for wanting to sell, you should tell them how useful that information is for you and that if they don't mind you have some questions of your own for them that will help. Ask them how long they have been thinking of making this move and what has prompted it to happen now? It is important to note that the questions you are asking do not have to follow my suggestions. The goal is to get the potential client to talk…and talk…and talk some more! Ideally, if your meeting is for one hour, the potential client should be talking for forty minutes of that. Only then will you be able to discover their real problems, which they need solved and explain how your service meets those specific needs.

From here you may also explain to them that before a property goes on the market it should have all the odd jobs completed and be professionally cleaned. When a viewing takes place, the property should be cleared of any clutter every time. Once you have agreed a price with someone, you will need to arrange a legal representative and communicate on a weekly basis. Someone will also need to speak with the buyer's legal team and the legal team of anyone else involved in the chain of buyers below. Once the legal work has been done, you will again need the home to be professionally cleaned. You will need to arrange removals to tie in with the few hours that you have free on the day of completion and of course, before that you will need to box up all of your belongings. The list can go on and on and on, until eventually you can tell them that although the other estate agents have told them they will sell their property, actually that is not what you guys do.

It does form part of what you do but actually, you move people - you do all of the above, specifically solving their problems and more - for one set cost and you only charge them when you find them a buyer who goes into a legally binding contract.

At the end of that process there is nothing to compare your fee with. Okay, the customer may still say; "Can you do it cheaper?" This is a normal question for people to ask, but you can stick to your guns, knowing there is nothing you can be compared with. If you have done this correctly you have left them with two options - heaven if they use you - and hell if they don't.

Having touched on that I'd like to say that productising your service and teaching you how to pitch is not what this book is about, we can save that for another book. What we are interested in is how do you find those dormant market customers in the first place?

We have explored interruption marketing, active markets and dormant markets so now the fun begins. We can look at how you attract new leads to your business by implementing a series of C words. Five words in fact and the first of which is; content. When we discussed interruption marketing I said it was a way of renting people's eyeballs for a short period of time, which has become more and more difficult to do in today's world. Now, we need to own their eyeballs.

# CHAPTER 4
## Content

**"They click to read or watch your content and for the whole time they are reading or watching your content they are purposefully choosing of their own accord to interact with your brand."**

# Owning people's eyeballs

The first C word in the successful loop of content marketing is, quite obviously; Content. Most businesses will have gone through the process of thinking up some sort of advert idea to draw in new customers in the past. These ideas are usually always based around using interruption marketing to find the small number of people who are currently in the active market for a product or service. This could be done through advertising a special offer or a voucher code. Alternatively, maybe an advert about how incredible your product or service is will be enough to tempt those active people into making contact.

There is no specific problem with this approach for immediate short-term gain and I am in no way saying this form of marketing does not have its place. But it is not reliable enough to drive the constant steady flow of new leads that businesses need for a long period of time to make the estate agency really stand out. It is more focused on short-term profit and loss, as opposed to long-term growth and success. It is like trying to win the war by only having enough soldiers to get through the first battle; eventually, you are going to run out.

# Engage, entertain, educate

In contrast to the approach described above, content marketing requires your business to create specific content, which is either, engaging, entertaining or educating - to the target audience - who your product or service appeals to. This is no strings attached content. There is no sales pitch involved in your content. Of course, the message is coming from your business, so in that sense there is a form of sales involved as the content is wrapped up in your brand. But the point is that you are not pitching for business with this content; instead you are offering something that you truly feel will be engaging, entertaining or educational to your target audience. It is a way of finding their 'wants' as opposed to their 'needs.'

For example, let's consider a gym or personal trainer. In their interruption marketing efforts, while trying to appeal to the active market they might have come up with some adverts based around a reduction in the joining fee to their gym; or a two-for-one price on personal training sessions; based on the needs of the service being cost effective. But with content marketing they would perhaps write a blog post about some simple techniques people can use to burn fat quickly; the potential customer's specific wants. Or maybe, they make a video showing how to use everyday items from around the home to create a personal workout. Now, this may on face value seem counter productive, after all, surely if someone already has fat loss tips or items around their home they can use to work out with, then why would they need the gym or personal trainer?

Content with engaging titles will draw more people to interact with your brand

The beauty of this is that in reality, the only people who are going to find that content appealing are those people who really want to lose body fat. Or those people who enjoy working out and as such, they click to read or watch your content. For the whole time they are reading or watching your content they are purposefully choosing - of their own accord - to interact with your brand. This in itself does not lead to a new customer, but it begins the process of brand loyalty and seeing your business as the experts they need. Sure, we still have a long way to go but remember; the longest journey starts with the first step. This first moment of self-chosen interaction with your brand is big, really big. These people did not happen to trip over your leaflet on their doormat, huff and puff as they bend down to pick it up and throw it away. These people actually chose to stop what they were doing and read or watch your content. If your content is good - entertaining, engaging or educational - they actually benefitted from that time they spent with your brand. Then they come away liking your business a little more than they did a few moments earlier, before they had seen your content and in some rare cases that one piece of content may even be all that is required for them to see you as the expert they need.

One problem I have heard repetitively from businesses that have made unsuccessful attempts at content marketing is; "But how do we create and keep coming up with new engaging, educating or entertaining content?" You are already busy right? You already have a million and one things to do, let alone turning yourself or one of your staff into some sort of ideas/writer/video producer. Then once you have all this content, who is going to do the administration of posting the content - across all the different media channels - emailing it or getting it designed for print? Well, the wrong answer is; "Anyone who is currently working for you" because they already have a job and unless you are already doing this part of the 5Cs process and that job isn't currently making content. They will be no more likely to be able to do that and do it well enough and regularly enough for it to work, than an accountant would be able to plaster a wall. You will need specialists and the smart way to do this is to outsource the work.

When clients of ours have often thought; "Hmm, maybe we can save some money and do some of this ourselves" it always falls down. The reason is not that they are incompetent, but simply that it is not their specialism and if it were, then they would be doing that job.

For example, a client of ours once made the point that they were spending £10,000 per annum with us on content writing. If they used one of their ladies from the office instead to write that content because she quite liked writing, they would make a nice, big saving. What they failed to take into account was that the said 'lady from the office' was on an annual salary of £28,000 and she already had a full time job. Even if writing all of that content could be done by taking up one third of her time, it would still be costing them £9,333 per annum. Plus the cost of the new person who was now going to be needed to pick up on the work that was no longer being done by 'the lady in the office.' Aside from all of that, they would no longer have specialist professional writers or videographers creating their content, but instead 'a lady from the office.' This not only leaves them with less engaging, entertaining or educating content, but also leaves them in a very sticky situation should the 'lady from the office' decide to go and work in another office or in another business.

The company in question implemented this change and although the lady did not leave to work at another company, within six months the move had not worked. At that stage, rather than going back to what had worked previously, the business pushed on with the 'in-house route' and decided to specifically employ a person for this role. The initial idea of making a huge saving of £10,000 had gone out of the window and they were now looking to hire someone on £30,000 per annum! Leaving them £20,000 per annum down on the original solution that had been working! Also, they faced the problem of how to attract a great content writer to a business that did not revolve around content writing. Anyone at the top of their game would not have applied or been interested because they all have aspirations of working in a business closely related to their own sector where there is a real career ladder. The person they did end up with only lasted four months and eventually they went back to the original plan and realised that spending the £10,000 per annum with us

- to have content professionally created on time in the right way - was actually, already the huge saving they were looking for.

## Where are your customers hanging out?

Now you have great content, but where will these people see this content? That is up to you and will depend on your budget. Social media is the most obvious place to start because using targeted advertising can make your content appear in front of exactly the right kind of person your content should appeal to and has been written for. This crosses the line between interruption and content marketing because although you are interrupting someone's social media, you are equally doing it with very specific content, which should appeal to that person's wants. Rather than generic adverts, which are fishing for the right people and annoying the majority.

As you reach more and more of these people with more and more good content - they will subscribe to your content - because they like it enough to actually want more of it. And slowly but surely you are building brand loyalty in people who do not yet realise they are going to buy your product or service, at some point in the future. Your brand and what you do is becoming imprinted on them. So, when the time does come, you can be pretty certain who will spring to mind for them. For estate and letting agents you can also look to put your content in front of people via print because working in a specific geographical location makes this easier to achieve. This can be done in the form of magazines or newspapers, but when using these outlets it is important to remember we need to be delivering engaging, educational or entertaining content to these people; not just putting properties and adverts about your business through their door. An example of this is a quarterly newspaper. It can promote properties and maybe contain a back page advert about your service, but the majority of the content should include free, practical information sources, such as: *What's on Guides for the area; Tips on increasing the desirability of your property; or Five ways to settle your child into a new school* etc.

For many businesses that is where their content marketing strategy ends. It is left as another of the marketing world's dark arts that is unquantifiable. Does it work or does it do nothing? Who knows, but who is daring enough to find out? Fortunately, I do not buy into that method of marketing and that is why I came up with the 5Cs loop. Once we are starting to attract people's interest we not only want to know who they are but we want to know what they are looking at and what interests them. Once we know what interests them then we can communicate with them and we can connect with them too by providing their wants and we can increase the level they like our brand even further.

## Success Story:
## Taking an aging brand to an expanded local favourite

John, from Petty Son and Prestwich had been in the estate and letting agency industry for many years before he took the plunge and bought an aging brand back in 2008. John's problem was not his own knowledge or his ability to do a great job, but instead the external image of the business that he now controlled. He engaged external experts to help him deliver effective content marketing by creating consistently great content and placing it on appropriate platforms to attract more customers by changing and upgrading their perspective of his business. This resulted in his business being known across the local area as 'The Estate Agent' to speak to. You only have to attend one of John's annual company events to see the huge support he has from his local community. Although a small business, John now has a well-structured and complete content marketing strategy. The reason that he continues to spend more on this side of his business is simple; it works!

# CHAPTER 5
## Communicate and Connect

**"The world has finished with untargeted, random adverts. Not only will it be difficult for you to pick up new customers using this method but the hidden killer is that you will actually end up turning far more people off your brand before they have even had the chance to get to like you."**

# How to annoy your potential customers

As explained in Chapter 1, most businesses think of their advertising as a way to tell people in an active market that they exist and they generally do this regardless of the consequences.

For example, if an estate agent wants to find home owners in their area who are thinking of selling their home they might send a leaflet to all the homes in the area telling them that they have a special offer for selling properties at the moment. Then, if the said estate agent gets one or two properties for sale from that campaign they would measure the success by that. But how about the damage; are they measuring that? If they sent out 30,000 leaflets and had one or two responses, what did the other 29,998 people who were not interested think about their business? This is very often ignored when measuring the success of a campaign. To measure long-term success you must also take into account damage. These people might need you later and you want to put credit in the bank rather than decrease your potential client base.

When email marketing first began to emerge as a real alternative to the postal service, it was only natural that businesses continued to think inside the box with their communication. If they had previously been sending out special offers or newsletters by post, they could now do that by email. It was instant and free and everyone rejoiced that the world had moved on. But in reality, the world had not moved on and nothing had changed because businesses were continuing to send interruptive marketing to people that had no interest whatsoever in the products or services being offered. The world had evolved; Yes, but moved on; No.

The most surprising aspect is that countless numbers of businesses continue to do their marketing in this way. In this chapter we will talk about how, if you haven't already done so, now it really is time to move on. Not only will it be difficult for you to pick up new customers using the untargeted, random adverts but the hidden killer is that you will actually end up turning far more people off of your brand before they have even had the chance to get to know and like you.

## How to deliver your content to the right people

In the last chapter we spoke about making sure your brand or business speaks to a very wide audience. Ideally, this is all of those people who are currently sitting in the dormant market for your particular sector.

To find these people you can use three main methods. Print, email and social media and for maximum effect you will use all three. To begin with you need to put your good content, that is engaging, entertaining or educational, in front of your potential audience. For some people this is easier than others because it depends on your particular sector. For example, if your business specialises in gardening, your potential audience are obviously people with gardens. Therefore, there is no point in having your printed material delivered to apartment blocks. You are simply wasting your money and annoying people who might have gardens later in their lives and one day might be your ideal potential customers.

With social media, this becomes even easier because you can filter down exactly who your adverts are appearing in front of, to make sure you are targeting your message to people who are likely to want to read or watch your valuable and useful-for-them content.

Going back to the gardener example, their printed material, social media or email campaign only goes to those people with gardens and the content is useful and practical rather than sales driven. For example, *Four quick tips to help you get perfect stripes on your lawn.* This will have a much higher success rate than; *We are the best choice for your garden. B*ut remember, it will have a much higher success rate based on the number of people beginning to like your brand because you give them useful and practical information for free - valuable content - as opposed to simply measuring the campaign impact by the number of direct enquiries.

Your potential audience will be pleased to have received your helpful tips in exchange for nothing in return. The Helpful Gardener is now seen as exactly that. However, this is not enough because to really connect with your potential audience you need to know who is reading your quick tips and which of them went on to read some further tips on your website or went on to look into how much you charge for your services. With this in place, you will then be able to customise your content and messages more specifically to their wants. Thus, pushing your potential customer further and further along your sales funnel until eventually they pop out at the end as a paying customer, but how?

Anyone familiar with traditional email marketing will know that monitoring the results is not quite as simple as it might sound. Having to log in and see who clicked or opened which content and segment those people out into new lists is painful at best and impossible at worst. The good news is that this is most definitely one aspect of the world that has moved on with the birth of new systems such as FRAGRA. This is a new email communication tool, which tracks and learns your audience's behaviour patterns and reacts accordingly.

Let's look at an example to put this into perspective. A nutritionist writes valuable content based on her expertise and targets it to what her customers ask her for, which means the nutritionist is responding to her niche market. Her content is entitled, *The secret to eating your way thin.* She pushes that content out to people on social media using specific targeting based around people who have shown an interest in the past in nutrition, dieting and health. She also places her printed version in a local gym and sends an email version to her existing database. FRAGRA watches those contacts from within the electronic communication network and sees what actions they take. The printed version will provide pointers for more good advice on her website, which will also bring those people into her tracking system.

Of the potential customers who read the content, some of them may go on to click on a related link on the nutritionists website entitled, *All you need to know about food intolerance testing.* This is an example of how FRAGRA now applies the interest of food intolerance testing against that particular contact. Once this interest has been applied FRAGRA knows how to put this contact into a predefined email series of content articles, videos and tips about food intolerance testing. But it does not stop there.

Now, the nutritionist knows this potential customer who was originally interested in how to eat thin, is also potentially interested in food intolerance testing. By connecting with FRAGRA, they can now offer a more customised website experience for that customer for when they return to their site, which we will be encouraging them to do because the nutritionist is now pumping out engaging, educational or entertaining content regularly, in order to bring them back to the site. When this potential customer returns to the website maybe they show a testimonial on the homepage about how the nutritionist helped a client eat themselves thin after a food intolerance test to work out their most beneficial foods to avoid.

However, at the same time another contact not yet known to FRAGRA visits the website for the first time where the homepage displays the usual full range of services. Different website users or potential customers see different content depending on whether FRAGRA has analysed their interests previously or not and if it has, it provides their specific interests more readily for them on entry to the website. This saves them time and gives them the information and valuable content that they are looking directly for without having to read content that is not aligned to their interests. A win-win situation!

## Be more appealing

It is through this kind of detailed connection with your potential customers that you will be able to drive up revenues. Not only in the short-term with quick fixes from the active market who want to take you up on your special offer, but with a long-term sustainable growth strategy. This can keep growing and growing as more and more people enter your FRAGRA online email tracking and nurturing system, from looking at your appealing content and revealing their particular interests.

The great thing is that the content you make is evergreen, meaning that over time you will end up with vast amounts of content that can be repositioned for all of your different needs. Also your tracking and nurturing system will continue to push potential customers along the road to becoming a paying customer with no hard sell involved. Even better than that because your fee structure has been planned out to make perfect sense and there was no hard sell or special offer, price will not be a deciding factor either because it is not the price that had driven them to you in the first place. It is knowledge and value, which is far more powerful and long lasting.

Firstly, we have now demonstrated how you can continually reach out to a wider audience with no hard sell by making more and more engaging, entertaining or educating content. Secondly, we have looked at how to communicate that content to the right audience. And finally, we have discovered how you can connect with your potential customers by learning their particular pain points or points of interest and automatically apply it to their profile in your data.

There are two steps left in the loop of the 5Cs methodology; Constant and Convert. In the next chapter we will look at what will be required for you to implement this in a constant manner and its importance, regardless of the size of your team. We will also discuss how by using this method, you can compete with any business, no matter the size.

# CHAPTER 6
## Constant

**"The problem with consistency in business marketing usually comes back to the fact that most marketing is based around a call to action. I call it; of the moment marketing."**

# Of the moment marketing

Here is how it goes…New business is drying up so a small amount of panic begins to set in. This prompts a brainstorming session designed to come up with that one killer idea, which will get lots of new business to walk through the door. The session ends with the brilliant idea of a special offer and then it is all guns blazing to get the message out. Sound familiar? Don't worry. It is in very basic terms a story familiar to most businesses.

The results of the brilliant new campaign will normally be measured by the number of new enquiries generated and from there the business can decide if it was a good or bad idea. If it turned out to be a good idea, which generated lots of new leads, the business won't need to have a new brainstorming session for a while. If it turned out to be a bad idea, which did not generate lots of new leads, then the panic will deepen and new, better ideas will be required!

Reading this scenario back to yourself sounds crazy doesn't it? With so many crucial aspects of business systemised and double-checked why is it that the marketing is so inconsistent, yet we expect it to work? Imagine if you were inconsistent about locking up your office each night or inconsistent in the delivery of your product or service? The results would be catastrophic; and your marketing is no different.

One of the most common reasons that inconsistent marketing fails is that businesses do not feel qualified enough to know what marketing they should and should not be doing. Also for many businesses, the marketing options are seen as an expense and there is a fear of wasting money or being seen as a fool. This in a large part is down to a fear created specifically by businesses trying to get you to choose their form of marketing. They give you all the reasons that you should use them for instant results and then when those instant results do not materialize, they tell you that your advert is not just for enquiries but for brand awareness and you will die without it.

This is another problem solved by using a combination of content marketing and an email tracking system. Nothing is left to the imagination. Using a tool such as FRAGRA you will be able to see precisely where all of your leads come from and you are not reliant on other businesses to find your customers. If people are not looking at your content, no one is to blame but you. Up your game, write better content or pay to have better content written. It is harsh, but also great for you because there is no set formula for your competitors to copy. They can implement the same techniques as you, but if your content is better - more valuable for your customers - you win.

## The nurture journey

The consistency of your new content can be taken care of by content writers. As your content is pushed out regularly, your tracking system will learn potential customer's interests and take them on content nurture journeys.

A nurture journey is a series of emails that have been pre-determined to take the recipient on a specific route dependent on their online actions. For example, you might decide that if a known contact clicks on the pricing page of your website, they will enter a nurture program that waits for one day and then sends them an email about how different people benefited from the specific service the page they clicked on talks about. From here you can send the journey off in two different directions. The first would be if the user clicks on the email and shows even more interest in that specific service; the consequence of that might be to move them to a different nurture program encouraging them to buy now or to notify a member of your staff who can contact them. The other direction would be if the recipient did not click on the email, in which case you might pause for ten days and then send another email to them about a different subject and so on.

To build these nurture programs you need a specific advanced software such as FRAGRA so you can simply drag and drop these nurture programs together to build your different routes and journeys.

## Stay on brand

The constant aspect of your marketing does not end there. It is also crucial that every part of your business is on brand. The constant reinforcement of what your brand looks like, the feel of it and the style of it, will need to be consistent for your messages to sell your business or service to your potential customers without having to repeat your company name again and again.

Whether you are reading this and running a huge multinational company or a small startup business, I cannot emphasis enough its importance. Not simply for the obvious aspects of your business, including your website, business cards and marketing material, but also for the notepads in your office, the pens the staff use, the contracts your customers sign. Everything you can possibly think of should be - on brand - and follow specific rules of design, which make that product stand out as yours.

This is also vitally important with your nurture messages. They must all follow a very similar format, not to the point where you can't tell the difference between messages, but so the long-term build up of seeing these messages sticks in the potential customer's head. You will not catch Coca Cola, Nike or Apple suddenly going off brand, using different fonts, colours and styles and why should you?

I highly recommend having a professional company look after this aspect - your branding - and any outward facing items of design from small items like company pens through to your advert campaigns. Apps and websites have made the software to do this job available to anyone, but the knowledge to do it well and having the time to do it for everything is quite a different matter. It is not an extra expense. It is an essential expense and part of running every business.

If you can take time and effort to get your brand right and be consistent with applying it, the difference that it can make to your business is far beyond anything you can imagine. Let me give you a great example of a story about a friend of mine who, for this purpose we will call Chris.

Chris wanted to be a hairdresser. He studied hairdressing at college and once qualified he went out into the big bad world to get himself a job. Luckily for Chris, his uncle knew a guy who owned a Barber Shop, called Chop Chop. It was a popular shop with the locals and had been there for more than fifteen years. However, during that time the front of the shop had fallen into disrepair. One of the Cs of the second Chop had fallen off, making the signage now read Chop hop. The paintwork on the front of the shop had also seen better days. Inside Chop hop, it was clean enough but there was nothing fancy about it. A mishmash of chairs made up the waiting area and the experience you received - from walking in until walking out - depended very much on how busy they were. At Chop hop, Chris charged £12 for a gentlemen's haircut and also picked up a bit of extra cash from small tips here and there.

After working at Chop hop for two years Chris received the bad news that the owner of the shop was retiring and the shop was being taken over by Toni & Guy. The new manager of Toni & Guy offered Chris a position at the new business and Chris accepted. The shop closed for two months while a team moved in to refurbish Chop hops into the new Toni & Guy.

Once finished Chris could not believe his eyes. Aside from the front of the shop looking super cool, the inside was like walking into a spaceship. On his first day back at work, Chris expected to go back to cutting hair, but instead he was sent on a targeted training course, explaining how to greet customers and how a hair consultation works. This process was followed for all members of staff - not so they did it like robots because they all used their individual personality - but the greeting and the consultation contained the same elements every time. Before long, Chris was charging £40 for a man's haircut and some of the ladies haircuts were upwards of £400. The tips were significantly higher too. How did that happen? Chris and his colleagues were the same, the service was the same, although more consistent, but the price had gone up nearly four times and Chris was busier than ever.

This brief story illustrates the power of getting your brand right at every single level of your business - from the outside attraction - to the welcome experience, to the ongoing communication and beyond. At Chop hops, the shop was screaming out cheap haircuts without even having to say it because that was the brand they were portraying. If they had upped their prices to £40 per haircut people would have laughed at them. But effectively a refurbishment and a more professional experience was all it took for the higher prices to be acceptable. It was the very same hairdresser doing the haircuts! Importantly, the new business had found their 'purpose'. They were no longer looking for anyone wanting a cheap haircut. Those people could go elsewhere. The business had found their niche and could now concentrate on finding and attracting, those looking for a more attentive experience. Once found, the prices were not an issue.

In this section, we have spoken about making sure you are consistent with both your content and your brand because these aspects of your business will be crucial in seeing the increase in revenue. But, to increase revenue you not only need to attract the right kind of leads to your business but also, you have to convert them into paying customers.

## Success Story:
## From mismatched multi-branch marketing problems to multi-award-winning market leader

Balgores were spread across five offices and were struggling to keep control of their brand. Individual branches were doing things slightly differently and there weren't any consistencies when it came to the design of items such as window cards and newspaper adverts. They were and continue to be a group of people with a lot of industry experience but were, by their own admission, struggling to get the right message across to potential customers. Balgores were chasing for business rather than business finding its way to them. They turned this completely around by working with external experts to introduce an effective content marketing strategy to their business across all branches. Their marketing and branding is now looked on regionally and nationally as one of the most impressive and recognisable in the industry. Nowadays, their marketing is structured and performing effectively and they have won more than 20 industry awards – whereas they had never won an award before - and they have expanded their business to eleven branches.

# CHAPTER 7
## Convert

**"What no longer works in today's world is employing a 'good' sales person and expecting him or her to simply drive faster, this may work when he or she is simply up against other 'good' or 'poor' sales people but once they come up against the methods I have outlined to you, in the medium to long-term, I am afraid there is only one winner."**

There is little point in going through all of the work involved in the previous chapters if your existing conversion process is lacking. Getting this aspect of your business correct is not more important than the other steps but it is an absolutely vital cog in the wheel of your business success and must always be seen as such. This aspect of the business must constantly evolve and develop and grow or risk becoming outdated. If you can think of your business as a Formula One team, this part is your engine and the work to make it better and better should never stop.

Most estate agencies feel that the number one issue when it comes to their conversion process is fees. In the previous chapter, we looked at the example of how Chop Chop hairdressers were converting customers based on a cheap price. They were eventually replaced by a more sophisticated business model, which charged four times the price. The result was they were busier than Chop Chop had ever been.

Before you think it, I know. "It is different in your line of business." Believe me, every single business, in every single sector says that. Even Chop Chop!

The main reason that most businesses never get past that problem is because they are not willing to restructure the solution they are offering. Therefore they continue to offer the same product or service as their competitor, with either a few extra or a few less bells and whistles attached to it and they fight it out based on price. Unfortunately, this only leads one way. Eventually, someone will undercut the undercutter and so on, until no one can make a living that way.

Lots of businesses also rely too much on the saying 'people buy people'. While I am not disagreeing with that statement in principle, it often leads to laziness inside the business. Going back to the Formula One analogy, it leads to the business not constantly refining their engine but instead constantly telling the driver to drive faster!

Once your business starts to put some of the processes in place that I am going to explain in this chapter you should feel a weight begin to lift immediately. Almost as if someone just turned the lights on. One client once described it to me as if he had just invested in Sat Nav for his business. In this chapter we will look at the processes that you need to have in place to ensure all clients that convert go through the same customer journey. We will look at methods that can be used to gather more data on potential leads/clients. We will also look at how you are delivering and tracking your market appraisals and giving yourself the best possible chance of converting them into instructions by using emerging technology to do so.

## The customer journey

The most important place to start with any conversion process and one that is missed by the majority of businesses out there is to actually map out the sales journey from the customer and your businesses perspectives. This can be one of those tasks that can give you a bit of a headache but stick with it. This alone, once completed will provide huge benefits to your planning, allowing you to identify the key areas that need addressing to tweak the engine.

To do this you must first know who your ideal customers are and then take a walk in your potential customers shoes. This needs to be done both literally, if you have a walk-in high street office and also in metaphoric terms for your website, social media accounts etc.

## Know who your ideal customers are

Before we take a walk in their shoes, who are they? This again, is something that has been made much easier to do with the explosion of Facebook. To start with you need to dig out the details of a client you have worked with previously, who in your eyes, was the perfect client to have. They paid the right amount of money, they were good to work with and they understood the process etc.

Now we need to profile that client. You can do this from all the details you already know about them but also, look them up on Facebook. You don't have to add them as a friend. On their Facebook page there is a More Button and in here you can see all of their likes, check-ins and groups etc.

From this information you can build up a huge profile on what your ideal customer looks like. Next, you need to list the three main goals that client had when they chose to use your service. For instance, for someone that uses a Personal Trainer the goals may have been: weight loss; gain better health; and to feel more energetic. Next, group those three details together and think of one overall problem that they were trying to solve. Like this...

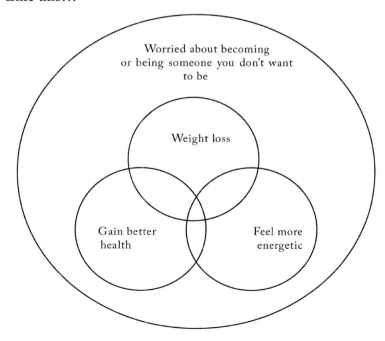

From here you can make an advert outlining that pain point and find your target audience, who you want that advert to appear in front of by using the techniques we spoke about in Chapters 2 and 3; by finding the same kinds of people through social media and offering them solutions to the same problem.

Now, as your potential new customer approaches your business you need to take a journey in their shoes. Back yourself up a hundred meters from your business, again in metaphoric terms, if you are not walk-in based. What does the potential customer see as they begin that journey towards your business?

What key messages, begin to start pinging in your ideal customers head based on the goals that you believe your ideal client is thinking of? If it is your website that they have first arrived at, what messages are screaming out at them and how do they relate to the specific goals they are looking to satisfy?

It is very common that - however great they are - many websites or shop fronts are screaming out about a product or service that the customer does not yet know is exactly the solution to their goal but using this model, you can know exactly what kind of customer is going to hit your website and tailor the messages to appeal to them.

Take a look at a well-developed and sophisticated business model such as BMW. Their website tells new visitors about, *Award-winning new cars, designed for your driving pleasure.* Also, on the homepage is their latest video, which states for example, *Adrenaline comes with four seats.* This specific video was clearly aimed at solving the goals of middle-aged men who want an exciting car but have to also accommodate the kids!

What they don't do is show their products on the homepage and expect people to know that this will be the solution to their problem or the goal that particular customer wants to achieve.

Have a good, distanced look at what the potential customer with those specific goals or problems sees when they first visit your business. Ask yourself this question; "Are they seeing the solution to their problem right there in front of their eyes or simply another shop front or website?"

"Is this a light bulb moment for them?" It damn well needs to be.

From here, you need to go through this process for each step that your potential customer will take on their sales journey - from start to finish - through to them becoming a paying client and beyond into long-term loyalty.

It is best not to over complicate the steps, keep them simple and chunk them down, one by one. You can break them down into more detail and with more choices, later.

At the back of this book I have listed practical resources, which you may find useful and one of these is a link to a template you can use to create this customer journey.

The key for each of these stages is to ask the following questions.

- What is the goal of the customer at this point?
- What is our goal at this point?
- How do we solve the customer's goals?
- How do we solve our goals?
- What resources are required?
- Which staff will be involved?

Answer each of these questions and it will automatically lead the customer along to Phase Two of the customer journey. Ask and answer those questions again and it will progress you to Phase Three. Keep going for each step and eventually, you will have mapped out your specific customer journey and exactly how your business goes about guiding your potential clients along your sales funnel into becoming paying clients and then continues to keep them happy beyond that right through into long-term loyalty.

## Use an effective measurement system

Another very important aspect to making sure you are constantly making those small improvements to your engine is to measure conversion rates. It sounds obvious but far too many businesses do not accurately measure how many of their hard earned leads convert into new business.

Without an effective measurement system, you can only guess at your conversion rates. When you have your customer journey correct and you measure your conversion rate, you can focus your attention on where improvements are needed on your ideal customer journey. When you do this, it will organically improve, often with immediate effect. This does not need to be a complicated system, but it does need to be accurate in terms of telling you the number of leads generated and how far they made it along your sales funnel. This way you can quickly identify any blockages and fix them to increase the flow.

You may also find, it is simply a case of having more suitable leads hit your sales funnel in the first place. If everyone is leaving at stage one, then either the wrong people are coming to the business or the initial messages the business is providing are not solving the right problems or offering the answers to achieve your customer's goals.

## Gathering data

At this point it is worth considering some form of quiz or report that your potential customers can complete to see how well they fit with your ability to solve their problems. These are sometimes called lead magnets. This will in turn give you the ammunition required to go back to them and address their specific problems.

To return to the BMW website, for example, if they had something on their website called, *The Car Genius - take our ten step wizard to find your dream BMW.* It would automatically provide BMW with all the information they require to put that customer on the journey to becoming a paying client.

For example, The Car Genius Test will ask you ten simple questions and recommend the perfect car for you. In this test, the car manufacturer can ask all sorts of questions that will help them in their long-term marketing efforts towards making you a paying customer. Question 1, might be how many children do you have? Question 2, could be pick your preferred budget; 20k - 30k, 30k - 40k, 40k+ and so on. Once the test or quiz has been completed your respondents will get the answer to the purpose of the quiz but more importantly all of that information that they have given you has been stored against their profile inside your automation system, such as FRAGRA. Using that knowledge your automation system will decide which marketing messages should now be sent to who; pushing potential clients further along the sales funnel automatically.

To put this into context of an estate agency, you might have a quiz or test on your website, which allows people to; *Find out the desirability of your home.* You can gather all kinds of data about people with questions such as:

- Is your property a flat or a house?
- Which of these price brackets would be the minimum that you would sell for?
- How much equity do you have in your property? And so on.

Following on from this example, you can reverse engineer that data to create a marketing campaign along the lines of;

*Do you own a semi-detached house? Do you have somewhere between, 100 - 150k equity and would you be looking to sell for somewhere between 300k - 350k? If so, we have the perfect solution for* you! Your response rate will be phenomenal because you already know that the answers to those questions are all yes; because they told you.

It is not magic. We appeal to specific people. We offer those particular people solutions to problems we know they are looking for solutions to. Then we reconfirm the problems we have solved for other people that happen to be exactly what we already know they are looking for.

What no longer works in today's world is employing a 'good' sales person and expecting him or her to simply drive faster, this may work when he or she is simply up against other 'good' or 'poor' sales people but once they come up against the methods I have outlined to you, in the medium to long-term, I am afraid there is only one winner.

## Delivering and tracking your market appraisals

Possibly the most important part of estate and letting agency business certainly in the UK, is winning the instruction. Such is the importance of this that this alone can be the deciding factor in a successful or unsuccessful business. This book is not designed to 'teach estate agency' but instead to teach and help already awesome estate and letting agents about the new methods of marketing and how they can be applied to their sector. Therefore, I will skip the patronising blurb about the importance of instructions and assume that knowledge already exists. If it doesn't, you have larger issues that need addressing before using any of the tactics from this book!

You or one of your team has been called out to complete a market appraisal. The long standing and ever so boring procedure goes something like this...

1. Book the appointment.
2. Visit the property and give a valuation along with a sales pitch.
3. Send the owner a letter or printed presentation detailing your thoughts.
4. Put the owner in the call back diary and hope to convert them to an instruction before any of the other agents.

I realise that some of you may have a few other bells and whistles dotted around that process but for the majority of agents, that is the crux of it.

Let's look at each individual stage and see how it can now be improved by more modern methods, then compare how the agent using those methods might fair against the traditional method we have already outlined...

1. Book the appointment - not much to really be changed here, it is what it is, but if the booking is made through your automation system, then step two becomes very different.

2. Visit the property and give a valuation and sales pitch - okay, this step is still going to be required but what if before this step your automation system has already began to 'prep' your potential new client? For example, if you book a test drive with Tesla the staff are trained to not book that test drive within one week from the date of enquiry. The reason for this is that they have a two stage prep program that will go out automatically via email. The first goes on the day that the appointment is booked and it is a video talking about Tesla as a company and their core values. The second arrives two days before the test drive date and is a video designed to build excitement and

enthusiasm for the test drive itself. Clearly, this is easier to do with the test drive of a car than a valuation appointment for a property but you can hopefully see the principle. It is a basic marketing principle, which states that it takes seven touch points with your potential clients to get them to buy from you. Using this method, by the time you visit the property you have already had three touch points and by the time you finish the valuation you will have had four.

3. Send the owner a letter or printed presentation detailing your thoughts. This is bad but a great example of how the estate and letting agency industry has not moved on enough in the last twenty years. To deliver your thoughts and valuation professionally, but more importantly in a trackable format you will need to use a tool such as the Bait tool from Iceberg Digital. You return from the appraisal, enter the details into the online tool and it will build your potential client a professional and slick looking webpage all about their property and your thoughts on it. Yes, this looks nice but the real beauty of it is that when your potential client is sent that presentation by email and they click to open it - they are now in your tracking and nurture system. Your tracking and nurture system will now not only notify you every time that owner is looking at their market appraisal but also every time they are on your website. Plus your touch points with the owner have risen to five.

4. Put the owner in the call back diary and hope to convert them to an instruction before any of the other agents. Step three has now also made this element look outdated. Of course, you still need a formal call back diary system of sorts but because of the previous step, not only will your valuer be notified whenever the owner is active on the appraisal website or your main website, allowing him/her to always have perfect timing for a follow up call, but also because your potential new client is now in your tracking system, they will be in a nurture program based on the status of the market appraisal. For example, if the status

is currently 'decision pending' we can rest easy knowing that without fail, the owner will receive your two stage drip program during the course of the next week, which would probably be testimonial emails from previous happy clients or success stories. Not only does this help you to ensure a smooth running system but guess what - it has taken your touch points up to seven - anything else from here is a bonus but now your potential client is ready to buy from you. From here they will go into longer term drip/nurture programs if required and your valuers will continue to get a notification or notifications when they are on any of your website be that in five days or five months.

Now, let's quickly compare those two methods...

## Traditional Method

1. Book the appointment.
2. Visit the property and give a valuation along with a sales pitch.
3. Send the owner a letter or printed presentation detailing your thoughts.
4. Put the owner in the call back diary and hope to convert them to an instruction before any of the other agents.

This gives your business a total of two touch points and they are now in the call back diary along with every single other valuation that has not yet come to market making it, at worst, impossible or, at best, very costly to stay on top of.

## Traditional + Technology Method

1. Book appointment through the automation system.

2. Automatically send a two-stage pre-valuation email campaign.

3. Send web-based presentation through the Bait tool which will notify the valuer when the owner is active on this or your main website, allowing them to always be in the right place at the right time to close the deal.

4. The Bait tool automatically places the owner into a short term and if required long-term nurture program, ensuring your continued and regular communication with them happens automatically and continues to encourage the owner to visit your website, which will in turn notify the valuer that their potential client is active and should be called.

Seven touch points and these will continue in the long-term nurture program if required. The call back diary becomes more manageable because automation is ensuring those that fall through the manual system are still in nurture programs with the relevant member of staff being notified if they need to take action.

Although some of this may seem too technical to some people or quite daunting, actually it is not. The companies that you invest in to do this for you should be more than familiar with helping companies in your specific sector to roll out these processes and systems and I say this from many years of experience of working in delivering technology based systems to the estate and letting agency sector. However, beware of working with good businesses that have no experience in your sector as it can very quickly turn into a nightmare.

The time for you to change is now; delaying it is only going to cause you more of a problem.

*"The only way to get rid of the fear of doing something is to go out and do it."*
**Susan Jeffers author, Feel The Fear And Do It Anyway**

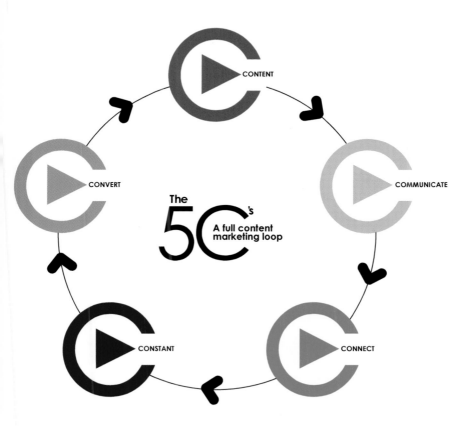

**How the full Content Marketing Loop works**

# CHAPTER 8

## Challenges

"Many companies have heard of content marketing but there are several specific problems that either; stop most businesses from doing it successfully or; stop them from starting on that journey."

The issues that stop it from working can usually be broken down into two main problems. The first is having the knowledge and skills and the second is the cost involved or the perceived value.

## Knowledge and skills

The knowledge and skills issue usually arises when businesses try and implement a content marketing strategy internally without outside help. This generally happens because the business owner or decision maker thinks it will be a more cost effective way of doing things. The key to making your business truly awesome is to have the best people working in or around your business. This is true in all aspects of your business, not only marketing.

However, all too often businesses are blinded by the thought that if they do things internally themselves they are somehow free. For this example, let's go back to the gym, where John runs a successful small gym and fitness business and employees eight people. You can replace the gym and fitness business with your particular sector. Although successful, John does not have a huge surplus of money at the end of each month. John wants his business to run better when he is not around so he can enjoy more of the benefits of owning a business. John finds himself having to get involved in all aspects of the business and when he goes away for a few days, he must check-in regularly to make sure everything is working well without him.

John has heard about this new form of marketing for his business; content marketing. On the face of it, the idea makes perfect sense to him. He continues to investigate the concept by reading books like this one. He visits a few seminars on the subject and also introduces Mary, his trusted administrator in the office to the idea for her thoughts.

Mary thinks it is a good idea too and would help them to gain more stability with their marketing efforts, rather than the peaks and troughs they currently experience with their more random approach.

John has no intention of hiring an entire new team to do this for him and he does not like the idea of outsourcing. How hard can it be, right? After all, John has already learnt that his content must be either: engaging; educating; or entertaining. He has explained that principle to Mary so they are all set!

Mary will write a new piece of content each week; John will check it; and Mary can post it to all their social media channels. Bingo! They will be delivering content marketing for the business.

In week one John says to Mary: "I have been thinking about this during the past few weeks and I think the perfect article to start with for our business is; *Four Tips on How to Lose Weight Fast*. Mary agrees but as an administrator in the business she is not sure what those tips are. However, this is not a problem because Mary will go and speak to Steve who as a Personal Trainer will have the tips she needs to write about. After a couple of days John asks Mary how the first article is going. Mary says she did try to speak to Steve but he was with a client and since then she has been busy sending the invoices out in time to meet the monthly deadline. But, she will speak to Steve again tomorrow and write the article for John.

Mary does not want to have to be chased again, so the next day she finds some time to speak to Steve when he is free and he provides the information she needs. Mary is quite a good writer and after a couple of days she has written the article and proofed it. She sends it to John for him to check.

John however, is booked out at meetings. He sees the email from Mary and is pleased everything has come together. He replies letting her know he can't look at it today, but will have a look tomorrow when he is back in the office.

The next day is a busy one for John, from the minute he gets in he is rushing around. He completely forgets to check Mary's article until near the end of the day. John opens the article and has a read through. He likes it, but wants to make several changes because he doesn't think it quite fits with what he has learnt about content marketing. However, he does not have time to edit it right now. He knows it needs to be done so he will do it later tonight at home. John completes his editing at home and sends it back to Mary for her to push out on social media and email the next day, which she does. Phew, a job well done!

## What happens now?

Firstly, for this to work it needs to be consistent. In seven days time, there needs to be another article going out. John's idea for the last article had come to him when he had been learning about content marketing, but he does not have another article idea ready and waiting. Mary does not have an idea to work on for him. So, John and Mary need to take some time out from what they are supposed to be doing to think of another article idea. Once that has been done they both need to catch up on their other work. Mary also now needs to find time to actually write that next article and going by the previous article that is not going to be instant or easy. John is actually finding himself reading and editing things in the evening now, so his idea that this would be part of him working less has never been further from the truth.

This cycle continues for a period of time with the gaps between new content being published getting bigger and bigger.

John and Mary have put so much effort into this that they never take a step back to realise that it is not being delivered effectively. There is no regular consistency to the content. The content is not always engaging, educational or entertaining because sometimes they are out of ideas. And crucially, there is no tracking system in place so the effectiveness of it cannot be measured. The critical questions are never answered, such as; how many followers did they have to start with? Has this number grown each week with each article? What feedback have they received? Has the article sparked any conversations and do they need to get back to people with answers, suggestions? There are no nurture programs in place for people that have shown interest in certain topics and the whole thing is effectively one big farce.

After a year, John decides this content marketing exercise is not worth the effort. It simply gets in the way of his and Mary's daily business activities and it doesn't do anything anyway! They are measuring their content marketing by how many people are picking up the telephone and buying things not from the online engagement they are generating from the articles provided. Therefore, the results are way below the required level for the business to continue with all of their hard work in creating this regular content. This has happened because they are not asking people for an instant sale in their content marketing. But instead they are hoping to bring them into their nurture programs, which will eventually turn them into customers. Without that in place they stop and John is right back where he started, working month to month on profit and loss and trying to come up with random marketing ideas as and when the cash flow needs a boost. John is no closer to being free of the day-to-day running of the business. In fact, he is further away from it.

## The cost or value problem

For an example of this problem, let's stay with John and his small business, but let's rewind.

John has heard about this new form of marketing for his business; content marketing. On the face of it, the idea makes perfect sense to him. He continues to investigate the concept by reading books like this one. He visits a few seminars on the subject and rather than trying to implement this by using his existing team, John decides to hire a new person to work specifically on this aspect of his business. Why? Because he believes it has value and will bring in more customers if it is delivered properly and with a dedicated driver to drive the program effectively, as their main focus, rather than as a side line to that person's other daily business activities.

John realises that although he likes the idea of content marketing, he is no expert. He places advertisements with recruitment agencies specialising in that sector. He searches for a content marketing guru and he sets his budget for a trial period of six months.

Now, John has an awesome business. His gym has won awards, the members are happy and John is a great business owner. But the problem John now has is how many content marketing gurus' have dreams that one day they might get to sit in a gym doing their content marketing?

This is not being disrespectful to John's business. They are awesome at what they do and they attract some of the very best people in their field. It is a fact of life that equally, most of the very best people in the content marketing field are going to have dreams of working for large marketing agencies on a variety of projects all at once, learning more skills with every project and moving their way up and up the ladder in their chosen field.

Because of this John, interviews people who no one else wants to do that job. I realise that not everyone will agree with this statement. Let's park that theory to the side and imagine that John does find his content marketing guru who he feels will suit his business and fit in well with his existing staff. For the purpose of this example, she is called Jane.

Jane knows exactly what John is trying to create. She has worked on projects exactly like this one previously and knows how the whole content marketing online loop works and the way to measure effectiveness of the software system they want her to use. She is perfect. The bad news is that the more Jane speaks to John the more she realises that John has underestimated the number of people he requires to make this work. While Jane is a specialist in content marketing, she is the equivalent of say, an architect and an architect cannot build a house alone.

Yes, the project needs to start and end with Jane but she is a planner. Jane explains to John she will need either a budget for outsourcing writers and designers or be allowed to hire some to help her. John trusts Jane's judgement and the business now needs to recruit great content writers along with graphic designers to make that content read and look really good. John also has to increase his original budget and starts to feel the financial pinch on the monthly profit statement.

From here things continue to grow because the content marketing section of his business is becoming a department in its own right and they require more administrators to deal with the content being created. They also need to make sure it is posted across all of the different social media accounts; including the website; and sent to print on time, to fit in with the planner's schedule and the content marketing strategy that they have agreed on with John and his business partners.

These key staff members will need the various new technologies we have spoken about in this book to be implemented across the business to measure who is looking at what content and following up with each potential new customer engaged with the content marketing process. Of course, not forgetting that each new staff member will also need the standard items of a desk, chair, computer, telephone, etc. After this staggeringly expensive recruitment stage, which John sees as a business investment, his newly set up team starts to work. John wants this to help him spend more time away from the business. He is pleased he has Jane on board because he relies on her to manage everything as she sees fit.

The loop is in place and everything begins to work. John is happy because he starts to see the benefits of the content marketing strategy for his business first hand. The problem John has now is that his outgoings have increased to astronomical levels. He has not only paid out the best part of £50,000 on recruitment fees for his new team but his wages bill has increased by approximately £15,000 a month.

Slowly, during the next year through the power of content marketing and its effectiveness to drive up revenue, John starts to begin to cover his new monthly expense. But then a hammer blow hits him!

Jane approaches John to say she feels she is doing a good job and asks for a salary rise. While John agrees about the work Jane has done, he does not yet believe he is covering all these new expenses on a monthly basis and it would be crazy to keep moving his break even goalposts further apart. Jane accepts John's decision but two weeks later tells him she has been offered a better job in an agency, which she cannot refuse.

While devastated, John knows his business has benefited from Jane's expertise and yet, he cannot do anything about the fact that his business is a stepping stone for Jane's fully fulfilled content marketing career.

Now John has big problems. He has no idea how this department runs because Jane set everything up. John needs another Jane and he needs that person quick. He starts the recruitment process again and meanwhile his new content marketing department is suffering from a lack of direction. The applications do not flood in for the position and eventually John makes a quick hire for the sake of having someone manage the department who knows what they are doing.

It is a disaster. The new Jane does not work the same way as the old Jane and wants to change the process and several staff in the team. Another member in the department resigns to go and work with Jane in her new job and John is firmly placed in his own business hell. Costs are out of control, he does not know what is going on in his business and he is working harder than before to control and manage this new situation effectively.

John is left with only one choice to save his business. The content marketing department is disbanded, immediately bringing his monthly costs back into the black. It is a short-term fix but the long-term damage is massive. The marketing has come to a halt. John has work to do to recover from the expenditure of the whole event and it is a 50/50 chance that he will be able to continue the business in a year's time.

On top of all of his woes, staff and technology move on fast. John needs pockets of money, deep enough to have everything in place because he might have started to see the content marketing loop working well, but the technology moves on slightly, leaving him and his processes out of date.

## The importance of your marketing strategy

At this point, you might be wondering what the whole point of this book is! We have explained the power and the benefits of having a complete content marketing loop in place, only to then show you how impossible it is to implement. But don't worry, there is a solution and you will learn how to do it in this book by reading on.

From the two examples in this chapter, you can understand why the idea of content marketing fails for so many businesses. They see marketing as something they can do internally themselves and then they wonder why it does not work properly. Let's not beat around the bush about this. For the marketing arm of your business to work, you have to take it seriously. In many people's eyes this is the most important section of your business, Without sales your business dies and without an effective marketing strategy those sales become harder and harder to come by. Sure you can blame increased competition, or the fact that one of your competitors is offering the service cheaper. But if you do not have a strong marketing strategy in place, you are not just struggling to stay with the game you are not even in the game. Ask yourself; "What is your marketing strategy?" Do you have one? Be honest with yourself; "Is the process you are currently using a bit random and based on luck rather than being a strategically planned out and effectively delivered plan of action, which you can afford, deliver professionally and measure successfully?"

Take a moment to reflect on these aspects of your business. If you know something different needs to be done for your business, then all I ask is that you give yourself the chance of success. Without a marketing strategy you are not giving yourself a fair chance.

## Success Story:
## From corporate to independent, solving the issue of having to do everything yourself

Neil King had previously been hugely successful in the corporate world of the estate and letting agency industry working his way up the ladder from Negotiator to Area Director of some of the country's biggest firms. Neil started his own agency back in 2004 and has never looked back, but something he struggled with from the beginning was the lack of support around him. The feeling of having to do everything yourself can be overwhelming, especially when you have pressing issues to deal with that simply cannot wait. Neil tried various ways to get his marketing under control from employing full time staff to managing it himself but it was always a problem area. He then went outside for professional help and invested in a real content marketing online structure and software platform. Neil's marketing has gone from strength to strength. Now, as the number one agent in his area, Neil remains mixed on his views about expansion, but he is fully confident that the marketing side of his business is under control and ready to be rolled out across new locations should he decide to go down that path.

# CHAPTER 9
## Effective Content Marketing Strategies

"Imagine if every single valuation for sales or lettings that your business has completed during the past five or ten years are still being communicated with automatically and they are in your tracking system, so you get a notification anytime they are looking at your website. You would potentially have all the business you would ever need sitting right there in your archive!"

# What is the solution?

Unless you know how to build and maintain a website you would not dream of building one yourself that you felt was going to stand up to the test of time for the long-term. Why would you think any differently about your whole marketing strategy?

The marketing arm of your business cannot afford to be seen as an 'add on' that 'we have a go at.' The strategy needs to be clear and the messages need to be consistent. There must be clear goals as to what your marketing is designed to achieve and complete clarity on the reporting side to monitor that the marketing is achieving its goals or if it needs tweaking.

For example, the typical agent would consider any property for sale in their geographical location - and even sometimes outside it - to be the business they want. While this makes perfect sense from a profit and loss perspective, in reality the types and choices of homes and types of sellers spread across that entire geographical location means that you are not specifically targeting anyone with your marketing. Instead you are simply sending random messages to the mass marketing hoping they appeal to someone, somewhere. As Patrick Lencioni, an American writer of books on business management, pointed out: "If everything is important, then nothing is." His analogy was referring to tasks within the business but the same can be said for your targeted marketing. Ask yourself; "Who are you targeting with the marketing you are doing?" This does not mean that you must restrict yourself to just one property type or one type of seller, but instead that you should create different messages for each. If some agent sends a random flyer to all of the properties in a specific block of flats saying; *We are an award-winning agent* and another sends something saying; *We specialise in selling flats, go to our website to discover the five reasons why we sell flats faster and for more money than anyone else can* - which agent do you think will get the better response?

These methods do not require incredible, groundbreaking meetings to change the entire direction of your business, but they do require you to stop blindly following the path of tradition and to peek your head up over the wall of estate agency and see how the world has moved on.

It is important that you are clear about knowing the marketing basics that you have learnt from this book so far to understand what it is that you are looking for in your strategy. We are no longer only creating marketing that will only appeal to the active market and calling on them to take action now. In fact we are only going to do that with 25% of our messages. The vast majority of our marketing is now focused on pulling more and more people into our tracking system to nurture them for sustained and longer periods of time.

Remember, we won't be able to draw them in, if our content is not engaging, educating or entertaining. The content, in this case, really is king.

## How it is done

Find the experts who can create your regular content - rather than hire a whole new internal department as John did in our last chapter - or have a go at it yourself. It is better to use a specialist group to make this arm of your business run effectively. This will solve the issue of you having to work late into the night writing articles, or for you to have to worry about if a member of that team leaves and needs replacing.

At this point you might be thinking; "But no one can really write about my business like I can; they don't have the knowledge" and you are right. But the point is that we are not looking to write about your business. We are looking to highlight the need for your business to create content that sits around the edges of your business to draw people in. To write great content for a lawnmower business I don't need to know the technical specifications of what makes the lawnmower work, but the best content writers can research and write; *The seven reasons why mowing the lawn quickly will make you a happier person!* It is important that you are happy with that content of course, but it is actually more important that it is being done and the process is happening; rather than worrying about every specific sentence in the content. If your content is being completed to a minimum of 80% - as good as you could write it yourself - that is good enough. The final 20% of effort will take up too much of your time to make any significant difference to the end results. This is best explained by the Pareto Principle, which originally referred to the observation that 80% of Italy's wealth belonged to 20% of the population.

More generally, the Pareto Principle is the observation (not law) that most things in life are not distributed evenly. In business for instance it relates as below.

- 20% of the input creates 80% of the result
- 20% of the workers produce 80% of the result
- 20% of the customers create 80% of the revenue
- 20% of the bugs cause 80% of the crashes
- 20% of the features cause 80% of the usage

In simple terms, use 20% of your time on a project to get it to 80% perfect and move on.

Writers working for clients to create their content are not working to create 'expert' advice that only they can give. They are working to fulfil the basic needs of content marketing; the Constant. Of course, as mentioned the content itself must be educating, entertaining or engaging, but the key on a very basic level is that it is being pushed out on a regular basis and there is a simple structure in place for doing that. Not one that will fall down and come to a halt if the flu bug hits the office or someone calls in sick.

Next up you need to make sure that content is falling in front of the eyes of the right people and for this you will need to use different types of social media. Facebook is the most obvious choice and is great for narrowing down your audience and paying to make sure the right content drops on the right people.

Also, it is important to make sure you use the tools made available by social networking sites to get that content in front of the right people. It may cost you to do this, but it will pay you back ten-fold if you have the whole content marketing loop in place. And once you have them in your tracking and nurture system, you'll never need to pay to reach them again!

The next step of getting this in place is to find the type of business you want to work with for your tracking and automation system. Clearly I am biased because I own a business, which has the FRAGRA tool in its suite of products, and specifically works in the estate and letting agency sector. But it is important to say not all tracking and automation tools work the same. You can be blinded by fancy screenshots and presentations about what a tool can do and often assume that it will do the basics of what you want. But all too often this is not the case. Time after time we meet businesses that have very sophisticated systems in place, but they struggle to do even simple tasks with it because it was not fundamentally created for their sector specifically.

Know the basics of what you want your tracking and nurture system to do and get the company you are considering using to demonstrate to you how you would achieve what you are looking for. It can be a disastrous and expensive mistake to assume that they are thinking the same thing as you when you explain to them what you want. To avoid this make sure they demonstrate the functions you require to see for yourself if that will fulfil your goal.

By investing in the right external experts you will not have to worry about staying on top of best practice or advancements in technology and you can do it within your specified budget.

However, the most important aspect of making sure the whole thing runs like a well-oiled machine is that all of these aspects must integrate together. Your content must be going out automatically across all of your social media channels and automatically being turned into emails that go out to existing clients and contacts without extra intervention needed.

Your social media accounts must be integrated into your tracking system so you can see a clear return on investment relating to each and every piece of content; Which channels did it work on and for how many people?

Also, your website and landing pages must be integrated with your nurture system to ensure that when a contact fills out a form they go straight into the right place in your system and automation can be run from the data they have provided. For example, if they say their eyes are blue in a form, how will that translate into your nurture system automatically and segment them into the blue eye list of people, automatically talking directly to them in the future about their stunning blue eyes.

The final part of making sure you have the full loop in place is to have a look at the convert process. This is the one part of the process that can be done effectively internally, as well as externally, but it can also be dependent on manpower. One particular issue that estate and letting agents have regularly with the convert process is that when attempting to turn valuations into instructions, their long-term nurturing does not exist.

The only attempt of this in the past has either been, a call back diary, which eventually is so full you have to cut the longer term prospects out, or some form of monthly email newsletter, which usually has uninspiring content and for the majority of the database does more to harm your brand than help it.

With the tools you have read about in this book you can ensure that you have tracking and nurture programs in place for not only short-term potential vendors and landlords, but for the longer term ones too. As well as this, you can have notifications set up to let the right members of staff know, at exactly the right time to call your potential new seller or landlords leaving no potential prospect unattended.

Imagine if every single valuation for sales or lettings that your business has completed during the past five or ten years are still being communicated with automatically and are also in your tracking system so you get a notification anytime they are looking at your website? You would potentially have all the business you would ever need sitting right there in your archive!

At the start of the book we spoke about how agencies used to be back when I started in the 1990s. The town I used to work in had six different estate agencies to choose from. I have run a quick search on Rightmove and there are now currently nineteen agents who cover the postcode my old office was based in. If I expand that search to agents within three miles, the results explode even further to more than five hundred agents! It stands to reason that not all of these companies can survive if there is not enough food to go round. By implementing the processes we have discussed in this book you can find the secret in your business and create your own unique kind of 'food' by removing the competition. Also ensuring there is a steady stream of new business (or food!) being created with a systemised and consistent process that does not require any panic meetings to get things done.

In the next chapter we can take a look into the future. Just for fun let's imagine the two scenarios - one based on implementation for all of the points we have discussed in this book - and one based on continuing to work in the way you currently do.

## Success Story:
## From an inconsistent marketing strategy to structured campaigns and x2 growth

Outlook Property Services are an established brand with multiple offices stretching across East and North London. Competition in their patch is as fierce as it could possibly be with super heavyweights such as Foxtons, Knight Frank and Savills, operating in and around their area. It is not just pressure from these corporates that squeeze Outlook though; some of the independents operating in the local area are equally as aggressive in their marketing. Outlook decided that they needed expert advice to help them put in place a more structured and efficient marketing strategy, as opposed to their previous more random approach. Their goal was to capture more of the sales market in their respective areas. The professional advice they received implemented various tools for Outlook that addressed their strategy issue and in turn grew their market share. The experts helped Outlook to get their entire content marketing loop off the ground, in online and printed formats and since that successful result they have also created the same structure for local marketing in individual branches.

# CHAPTER 10

## Agent X; What will the estate and letting agency look like in five years?

Before we start this final chapter - a look into the future - I want to put things into perspective for you. For some people who have read this book, it may feel that the items covered are already too futuristic for them to absorb. To avoid you feeling that maybe some of this is pie in the sky material or it will never happen, let's look at the reality of what is really happening in the world of technology to put this into context.

# Perspective

Dave Evans, Cisco's chief futurist and chief technologist for the Cisco Internet Business Solutions Group (IBSG) spoke to Network World (www.networkworld.com) about his home as an example of the speed of network improvements. Network performance has increased by 170,000 times since 1990, when he had only one telnet connection. Today, Evans has 38 always-on connections (smart phones, tablets, televisions etc.) and more than 50Mbps of bandwidth, enough for tele-presence, streaming movies and online games all at the same time.

During the next ten years, Evans expects the speed to his home to increase by three million times. While most of the industry is focused on 40G and 100G, whole new forms of networks are also being created. Vint Cerf discusses the new protocols needed to build an interplanetary network, which can send data vast distances without being disturbed by latency. Evans notes that multi-terabit networks using lasers are being explored and early work is happening on a concept called; 'quantum networking' based on quantum physics. This involves 'quantum entanglement' in which two particles are entangled after which they can be separated by any distance, and when one is changed, the other is also instantly changed.

Production quantum networks are likely decades in the future, but it hopefully helps to bring us all back down to earth about how straightforward the items we are discussing are and how real the dangers are of simply standing still with your current strategies.

# In five...ten...fifteen years time

For this exercise I need you to have a little faith. The process is a little 'hippy' but all I ask is that you allow yourself to feel the benefit and try it out wholeheartedly; you have absolutely nothing to lose and everything to gain, so why not? To do this you will need to find a quiet place, away from noise and distraction where you can be left alone for the next ten minutes.

To start with we are going to go into the future, based around the idea of not changing anything at all in your current business. This is not a 'hopefully it will be like this' exercise - this is if nothing changes. Sticking with the methods that have got you this far and continuing with them. I want you to clear your mind and picture what your business might be like in five years time. Take some thinking time after each bullet point before reading the next one.

- Are you working harder or is life easier?
- Have your annual revenues and profit increased or decreased?
- Is your business thriving or are you struggling?
- How is your home life?
- Are holidays difficult or easy to take?
- Do you think new players will have entered your specific market?

Now, keeping those thoughts in your mind move it on a whole extra five years.

We are now ten years into the future and none of your processes and systems have changed.

- What will the date be?
- How old will you be?
- How does your business look now?
- Are you still even in business?
- How is your work life balance?
- Are things running smoothly and has all of your hard work now paid off?
- Or are you still trying to find the magic ingredient?
- If you have children, how old are they now?
- How do they see you at this point?

Lastly, I'd like you to imagine fifteen years from now.

- How do things look?
- Is it all roses in the garden or is it not a good place?

Take some time; really picture your business fifteen years from now, without change. What year are you in? Has your business survived?

Now, bring yourself back to the present. Think about all that you have read in this book - from right back to my early days, running around as a junior negotiator - through to the expiration of interruption versus content marketing. How you can now look for the different angles in your business to remove the competition?

Think about your business having the principles of the entire content marketing loop in place. Your content goes out on a weekly basis right across social media seamlessly and your tracking and nurture system constantly communicates with any and all leads that have been placed on your system during the past five years, alerting you when any of them are starting to become active again. Your marketing and branding run like a tight ship and work regardless of whether you are in the office or on the golf course. Your leads are all managed in the same way every single time and every customer goes through the exact same customer journey from enquiry to five star testimonial, happy clients. Not by chance, but because everything has been planned out and works to a system, allowing you not only to thrive in your local town, but to expand and grow the business. Due to having these systems in place the business has not only become more profitable but the exit value of the business will have also gone through the roof, due to the fundamentals of the business running like a well-oiled machine regardless of you being present or not.

Now, let's do the same exercise but imagine yourself in the business we have just described.

- Clear your mind and picture what your business might be like in five years time.
- Can you see a real direction for the business?
- Has it become easier for everyone to work towards specific goals?
- Are you excited again about this business?
- Does it feel like the business will be thriving or in decline?

Now keeping those thoughts in mind move it on an extra five years. So we are now ten years into the future the systems and processes in this book have been in place for many years and you have mastered them as a business. The companies that you work with have been keeping abreast of new and emerging systems too and your business has remained at the forefront of these changes. What would the date be? How old would you be? How does your business look now? Perhaps you have sold the business? How is your work life balance? Are things running smoothly and has all of your hard work now paid off? Or are you still trying to find the magic ingredient? If you have children, how are old they now? How do they see you at this point?

Lastly, I'd like you to imagine fifteen years from now.

- How do things look?
- Is it all roses in the garden or is it not a good place?

If you did that process with the right amount of effort then I can tell you now, you are awesome. Most people are too scared to even take that mental journey, let alone actually implement the change.

It is an interesting exercise. I obviously cannot be sure about what you saw on both journeys, but it is well worth writing it down in the table provided below. This will allow you to stay focused on why you are doing what you are doing; be that sticking with what you have or making the change.

| Number of years into the future | How were things if no changes to the business? | How were things if the business has implemented the changes contained in this book? |
|---|---|---|
| Five | | |
| Ten | | |
| Fifteen | | |

The power to change your business is in your hands. You have read all of the information. You have visualised the difference it can make. Now it is up to you as to how important you think that change is to make. It can be made today, tomorrow or in ten years time. I urge you to seize this opportunity to shift your business, I cannot tell you it will not have its troubles along the way, but I can tell you it will be an incredible journey - to sit at the front of the ship - as the estate and letting agency industry enters a new dawn.

My business, Iceberg Digital, can help you with some of the things you need to do, but not all of them. I personally can help you with some of them, but not all of them. Some actions and strategies can only come from the founder, the visionary of the business. Our industry is on the dawn of something very new and very exciting, I hope you feel enthused and ready to kick some ass, making sure your business is one of the few that will lead the way. Good luck.

# Final task

Now that you have a good understanding of what is required to get a full Content Marketing Loop in place for your business, as a final task I'd like you to rate your business using the following score charts. There is no point in doing this and trying to justify a good score simply to feel better. It is very important that from what you have read, you are now honest about your current situation because only then can you move things forward and see improvement. Once you have completed this task, then you can speak to companies that can help you improve these individual items and revisit this list every three months to update it and make sure it is always either improving or running at max power.

# The 5Cs Table

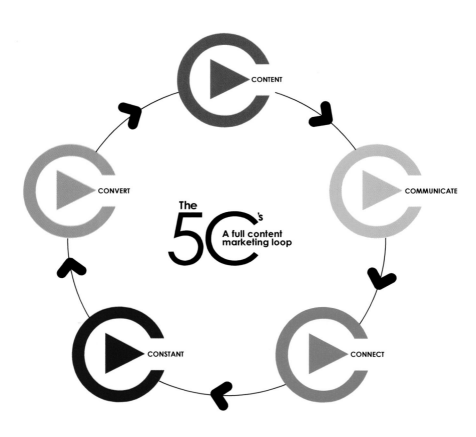

# Content

Are you creating, regular - weekly or more - engaging, educational or entertaining content, which is stimulating your audience?

(Tick the relevant box)

| | |
|---|---|
| Poor | |
| Average | |
| Good | |
| Outstanding | |

# Communicate

Are you communicating regularly - weekly or more - by using your engaging content with your existing customers and with new potential customers via email, social media channels and in print?

(Tick the relevant box)

| | |
|---|---|
| Poor | |
| Average | |
| Good | |
| Outstanding | |

# Connect

Are you connecting with your own existing customers and with new potential customers by gathering data and keeping a track of their specific interests and activity from your website and mailing them only about items that relate to their needs?

(Tick the relevant box)

| | |
|---|---|
| Poor | |
| Average | |
| Good | |
| Outstanding | |

# Constant

Is your brand consistent in **everything** that you push out to the world, in terms of marketing collateral, social media, content, etc.? Is it completed using an automated seamless process, which would continue to run regardless of if you were in the office or not? Or is it a bit random?

(Tick the relevant box)

| | |
|---|---|
| Poor | |
| Average | |
| Good | |
| Outstanding | |

# Convert

Do you have a process in place for your business, which is nurturing potential customers and highlighting **when** you should be converting leads into customers, making sure you are always in the right place at the right time, or is this done solely by call back diaries?

(Tick the relevant box)

| | |
|---|---|
| Poor | |
| Average | |
| Good | |
| Outstanding | |

**Mark Burgess can be contacted in any of the following ways.**

**Website:** www.therealmarkburgess.co.uk
**Email:** mark@iceberg-digital.co.uk
**Facebook:** www.facebook.com/mark.burgess.524381
**LinkedIn:** www.linkedin.com/in/mark-burgess-ba905419
**Iceberg Digital:** www.iceberg-digital.co.uk

iceberg **products:**

**Gabble; content writing**
Providing content writers dedicated to your business who will come up with educating, engaging and entertaining content for you on a regular basis, without you having to worry about how to do it.

**FRAGRA; marketing automation and tracking system**
FRAGRA is marketing automation that uses tactics. Prospects are targeted, based on their activities and receive specific content and marketing, thus nurturing them from first interest through to sale.

**Bait; attract and net your prospects**
After a market appraisal has taken place, you return to the office and enter in specific details such as, valuation, comparables and unique property insights into our system. The Bait tool

builds a beautifully presented website using the information entered showing that you are a cut above the competition.

FRAGRA tracks your potential client's activity, alerting your valuers whenever a potential client is looking at their market appraisal, or any page on your website. You will know how active a potential client is and when is the right time to contact them.

Based on the status of the market appraisal, FRAGRA will automatically pull the potential seller into a pre-built drip/ nurture email journey, pushing them through the sales funnel.

**Any Ideas; graphic design agency**
Design agency helping your brand live up to its potential. Keeping your marketing always on brand and bringing your projects and adverts to life through creativity and flair.

**Lambuka; drag and drop together your own branded magazines and newspapers etc.**
Automatically pulls in your live property data from your inhouse software, allowing you to simply drag properties onto pages and create stunning printed and digital magazines and newspapers in an instant.

## Hunt: Putting the right info in front of the right people in Facebook

Used in connection with FRAGRA, Hunt takes orders from FRAGRA about what your contacts and potential new clients are interested in, then tracks down their profiles within Facebook and generates bespoke adverts that are only relevant to them to target those contacts, leading them back to the conclusion that your company is the right choice for them.

## Campaign: Automating the process of beautiful monthly newsletters

Monthly email newsletters are great but the process of putting them together each month can be a pain. Campaign automatically sucks up the content that has been created for you each month by Gabble and designs it into a stunning monthly newsletter, then emails it out to the database on a set date each month without you ever lifting a finger.

## SOLNY: Keeping people informed of properties you have Sold or Let near them

This tool works in connection with Bait. The Bait tool knows the location of each and every market appraisal that you have attended and if they are still decision pending or have instructed another agent. What SOLNY does is keeps track of any properties that you mark as SSTC or Let in your estate agency software, then checks to see if those properties are within a 1 mile (can be adjusted) radius of any potential instructions within Bait and sends them an email informing them that you have Sold or Let another property near them. It also creates the printed artwork for you automatically should you wish to order flyers for the surrounding properties.

**Kickback: Automatically respond to your incoming enquiries**
Kickback is an auto responder that you can set up to instantly respond to enquiries that come through to you from sites such as Rightmove. Kickback will send the enquiry back an email automatically thanking them and letting them know that someone will be in contact shortly, and perhaps pointing them to other useful content on your website.

**Estate Agency X: The future of estate & letting agency**
Estate Agency X is all about information, support and helping traditional estate agents to adapt their business to the modern world through regular events, podcasts, videos, and blogs. Estate Agency X will challenge the way you think about every part of an industry that you thought you knew and gets you reinvigorated with new ways to make your business even more awesome.

**All products brought to you by Iceberg Digital**

# Useful Resources

Useful resources on the web or business books in print.

**www.uxpressia.com**

Visualize your customers' journeys with CJM Online Tool. Find all pain points and barriers in your service and turn them into advantages. Analyze customer journey step by step and get insights. Share. Inspire. Improve.

*Traction: Get a Grip on Your Business* **by Gino Wickman**

Discover simple yet powerful ways to run your company that will give you and your leadership team more focus, more growth, and more enjoyment.

*The E-Myth Revisited: Why Most Small Businesses Don't Work and What to Do About It by* **Michael E. Gerber**

An instant classic, this revised and updated edition of the phenomenal bestseller dispels the myths about starting your own business. Small business consultant and author Michael E. Gerber, with sharp insight gained from years of experience, points out how common assumptions, expectations, and even technical expertise can get in the way of running a successful business.

*Zero to One: Notes on Startups, or How to Build the Future* **by Peter Thiel**

The great secret of our time is that there are still uncharted frontiers to explore and new inventions to create. In Zero to One, legendary entrepreneur and investor, Peter Thiel shows how we can find singular ways to create those new things.

**www.gliffy.com**

Gliffy is a great tool to create various types of diagrams from network diagrams to customer journeys.

**www.valpal.co.uk**

ValPal is an instant online valuation tool that sits on an agents' site and converts their web traffic into vendor and landlord leads and feeds them directly into your FRAGRA nurture journeys.